Choosing & Sorting Your

∼ Pearl Beads

True natural pearls are jewels from the sea, the lake or the .... and costly. The demands of fashion from Tudor times to the present day ha............ ....ation to the bead industry and costume pearl beads are now made from many materic.. with different types of finish and in a multitude of sizes and colours.

Plastic -these are the least expensive pearls - they tend to have slightly bigger holes than the other types but the pearl effect is often grainy. They are very lightweight which can be an advantage if you are using bigger sizes.

Glass - these are a medium priced bead. The glass takes an excellent pearly finish which can be dyed very successfully in all shades from a subtle ivory to vibrant primaries and a reasonable black. The quality of glass pearls can vary - watch out for heavy pearl coatings that pull away at the holes or thin coatings that scratch easily. All of the samples in this book are made from glass pearls.

Shell - Premium fashion pearl beads are made on a shell or mother of pearl base - they are wonderfully lustrous but quite expensive. For extra-special projects only.

Pearl beads have an entry and an exit hole left over from the manufacturing process. For quick and easy threading pass into the bead where the pearl effect seems to fall into the hole and out of the other hole where the pearl effect will seem to flare away from the bead.

∼ Crystal Beads ∼

'Crystal' used to mean a bead made from the semi-precious stone known as Rock Crystal, but nowadays it means a bead made from a crystal quality glass. This glass is able to take a finely detailed faceted shape with a very shiny polished finish.

Historically, glass crystal beads came from Austria or the Czech Republic but very good crystal is now being made in China, India and Turkey. All of the crystal used in this book comes from China.

Crystal beads come in many shapes and sizes - this book uses two sizes of crystal rondelles but you can substitute for similar sized beads of a different shape if you wish.

∼ Chatons ∼

These pointed back diamante stones are available in many sizes - this book uses 3.5mm and 4mm foil backed stones for maximum sparkle.

Stick the stones into the mounts with PVA glue - when it dries it is clear and a little flexible which is perfect for making jewellery.

crystal rondelles

crystal bicones

crystal rounds

Tips & Techniques

There are a few basic techniques that you need to make the projects in this book. Even if you have made beaded jewellery with wire, links, crimps and beading wire before read through the information and try out the techniques first - a little practice goes a long way. There are tips for getting a professional finish and getting the most out of your supplies.

1 To make a round loop you will need to use a pair of round nosed pliers. The noses of these pliers are cylindrical and taper to a point. Depending on where on the nose you wrap the wire you will get different sizes of loop (fig 1). The designs in this book require smaller sized loops approximately 3mm in diameter.

fig 1

2 To practice your loops use a headpin. Thread on a seed bead, a pearly bead and a seed bead. Trim the wire to leave 8mm of wire showing at the top (fig 2).

Making a Loop

To make dangling drops, chain links and pendant pieces you will need to make a round, securely closed and centralised loop at the end of your wire or pin.

fig 2   fig 3   fig 4

fig 5

5 You are aiming to make a centralised, closed loop. The top of the loop should be directly above the main stem of the wire (fig 5) - if you need to make adjustments use the very tips of the pliers. Practice five or six times until you get more confident.

3 Using the tips of the pliers grip the pin immediately above the top bead and tip back to 45° (fig 3).

4 With your free hand hold the beads on the pin firmly. The end of the pin will swing around - bring the cut end to point at your chest. Grip the very end of the cut wire with your pliers 3mm from the end of the tool nose. Roll the wrist of the hand holding the pliers away from yourself to form the loop (fig 4). Make sure the loop has closed.

Beader's Tip
Be frugal - if you are trimming more than 20mm of wire from the top of your pins save the trimmings. Use them instead of eyepins for small links. Save money and the Planet!

Opening and Closing a Loop on a Pin

For extra fluidity several of the designs in this book link headpins to eyepins (loop-ended pins).
First - make a complete loop at the top of the first part of the bead sequence.
Second - grip the eyepin loop with your pliers at 90° to the stem of the pin. Hold the base of the stem as close to the loop as you can with your other hand.
Third - twist the loop open gently by rotating your plier wrist - don't pull the loop open - just twist it open sufficiently to insert the prepared link. Thread on the prepared link.
Fourth - put the pliers and your other hand back in the same position and twist the loop closed.

Making Loops Work Together

If you make a loop at both ends of a pin you need to make sure that the loops are in the same plane as one another (fig 6).

fig 6

When you link up to the next component the join will be smoother. If you are making a chain of links this is especially important to get a good 'fall' and fluid movement along the length.

Making the Loops in the Same Plane

Make the loop at one end of the wire and thread on any beads you require. Trim the wire if necessary. Hold the wire directly in front of yourself with the cut end of the wire vertical and the loop at the bottom of the pin in the opposite plane to your body. Place the pliers on the wire and roll the loop away from yourself.

If you need to adjust the plane hold across both loops with two pairs of pliers - when the handles on the pliers line up (fig 7) the loops are in the same plane.

fig 7

Making a Link with a Jump Ring

Jump rings are used for linking together components into chains, bringing together the strands of a tassel, attaching clasps and adding extra articulation where somethng needs to move freely.

Jump rings must be opened and closed properly to maintain their shape and strength. Just like the loop on an eyepin a jump ring is twisted, rather than pulled, open. It can be a bit fiddly as there is so little to hold onto so you will need to use two pairs of pliers. Practice with a larger sized jump ring and follow the directions below. You will soon 'get the knack'.

For right handers - hold the jump ring vertically in front of you with the gap at the top point towards noon. Grip with your first pair of pliers at 3 o'clock. Bring the other pair of pliers up from the 6 o'clock direction but grip the ring to cover 7 o'clock to 11o'clock (fig 8). Hold the left hand pair of pliers still and roll the right hand pair away from you to twist the ring open (fig 9). Pop in the components you need to link together and place the pliers back on the ring as before. Roll the wrist back to close the ring.

fig 8

For left handers - reverse the diagram and hold the first pair at 9 o'clock and the second pair to cover 5 o'clock to 1 o'clock. Roll the left wrist to open and close the ring.

fig 9

Using Stranded Beading Wire & French Crimps

Stranded beading wire is strong, flexible and easy to use. It can be covered with beads all the way around - which you can see in the Waterfall and Artemis necklaces or dotted with beads in a 'floating style' as in the Juno and Gloria designs. Treat the wire with care - it can kink if you get into a tangle. Keep it smoothly wound onto a reel when not being used.

French Crimps

Stranded beading wire is not finished with a knot but with a special crushable bead called a French crimp. Crimps are tiny metal beads or tubes made from a soft metal tape.

To squash French crimps you will need a pair of flat faced pliers (chain nosed, flat nosed or snipe nosed) or a pair of crimping pliers.

Flat faced pliers simply squash the crimp onto the wire - you can use these pliers with any size of crimp.

Crimping pliers crease and fold the crimp into a neater shape but you need the right size of crimp to match with your crimping pliers.

Practice makes perfect - try out your pliers on a scrap of wire first to get used to the technique. Thread a crimp onto the stranded wire. Push the crimp up against your thumbnail to hold it steady and squeeze the crimp. The crimp will crush easily - don't use too much force and take your time. If you rush the pliers will slip off the crimp, the crimp will twist, not hold the wire properly and you may kink the wire. If you are using flat pliers use them quite close to the hinge - you will get more control of the squeezing action.

1 Cut sufficient wire for your design allowing at least 80mm extra at each end for finishing the length. Thread on your design.

2 Thread a French crimp onto one end of the wire (fig 10). Bend the end of the wire back towards the end of the design passing it through the crimp to make a loop (fig 11).

Making a Loop at the End of a Beaded Design

fig 10

fig 11

fig 12

fig 13

3 Making sure that the beads are not falling off the other end adjust the size of the loop until it is 3mm in diameter. Squash the crimp to secure the loop.

4 Push the beads of the design up to the crimp concealing the cut end of the wire inside the first few beads (fig 12).

5 Thread a crimp onto the other end of the wire. Make a loop as before passing the wire back through the first few beads of the sequence (fig 13) and squash the crimp. Carefully trim off the excess wire.

Making Floating Style Designs

The French crimps can be used to secure beads at intervals along the stranded beading wire. The crimps need to be squeezed into place very carefully so take your time - you will need this method for the Gloria and Juno designs.

1 Layout the beads you want on a flat surface. You will need an extra bead for each end of the wire to support the loop - check your design instructions to see what you need to use.

2 Cut a length of wire 100mm longer than your required finished length. Thread on one crimp, one of your end beads and one crimp (fig 14).

fig 14

fig 15

fig 16

fig 17

3 Bend the end of the wire back through the last crimp and into the end bead not out the other side of the bead) to form a loop (fig 15). Adjust the wire until the loop is 3mm in diameter and squeeze the crimps to secure (fig 16).

4 Thread on the main beads for your design with one crimp on either side of each bead (fig 17). DO NOT SQUEEZE THE CRIMPS YET

5 Thread on one crimp. Position the crimp 10mm short of the final finished length and squeeze to secure. Thread on the second end bead and a crimp. Bend the wire back through the last crimp and the bead. Pull on the end of the wire to bring the loop down to size and squeeze the last crimp to secure (fig 18). Trim off the excess wire carefully.

fig 18

6 You can now return to the beads along the length - check with your design instructions before you squash these crimps to secure the beads.

Making Twisted Wire Designs

The Juno and Artemis designs use 0.4mm continuous wire to create twisted stamens and petal shapes from seed beads and pearls. The success of the design will depend on you getting the twists even and in the right place - much of this is achieved by holding the wire correctly with your other hand.

Making The Twists

Thread on the bead or beads that the design requires. Pinch the two sides of the wire together where you want the base of the twist to be (fig 19). Turn the bead or beads over and over to form the twist - if you tension the wire between your hands a little as you twist the result will be more even.

fig 19

Clusters of stamens all need to join up at the base so make sure your twist goes all the way down to meet the bottom of the previous twist (fig 20) - if it doesn't the design will not be firm.

fig 20

Beader's Tip

You need to use a soft wire when you are making twisted designs. As you turn the wire over and over to form the twist it stiffens up a little - don't over-twist as the wire will become brittle and break.

Waterfall Necklace & Earrings

A simple design made stunning by the use of pearls and crystal beads. You can make the strands a little longer, or shorter, if you want by changing the number of links. Refer to pages four, five and six for extra information on loops, linking, jump rings and stranded beading wire.

You Will Need

2g size 10/0 seed beads A
4g size 3 bugle beads B
Thirty-three 4mm pearl beads C
Twenty one 6x4mm crystal rondelles D
Eight 6mm pearl beads E
Three 6x8mm crystal rondelles F
Thirteen headpins
Twenty-two eyepins
Fifteen 4mm jump rings
60cm of stranded beading wire
Two French crimps
One clasp set
One pair of earfittings

Making the Necklace

1 Thread onto a headpin 1B, 1A, 1C and 1A. Trim and make a loop. Make nine of these links in total and call them P (see fig 21).

2 Twist open the loop on an eyepin and attach 1P. Twist the loop shut. Thread on 1A, 1D and 1A. Trim and loop. Make seven of these in total and call them Q (see fig 21).

3 Twist open the loop on an eyepin and attach 1Q. Twist the loop shut. Thread on 1A, 1E and 1A. Trim and loop. Make five of these in total and call them R (see fig 21).

4 Twist open the loop on an eyepin and attach 1R. Twist the loop shut. Thread on 1A, 1F and 1A. Trim and loop. Make three of these in total and call them S (see fig 21).

5 Twist open the loop on an eyepin and attach 1S. Twist the loop shut. Thread on 1A, 1E and 1A. Trim and loop. Call this dangle T (see fig 21).

6 You should now have nine dangles (fig 21). Attach a 4mm jump ring to the top of each dangle.

fig 21

7 Thread 1A onto the stranded beading wire.
Thread on 1B and 1A four times.
Thread on 1C and 1A.
Thread onto the wire 1B and 1A four times.
Thread on 1C and 1A.
Thread onto the wire 1B and 1A three times.
Thread on 1C and 1A.
Thread onto the wire 1B and 1A two times.
Thread on 1C and 1A.
Thread onto the wire 1B, 1A, 1C, 1A, 1B, 1A, 1C, 1D, 1P, 1C, 1D, 1Q, 1C, 1D, 1R, 1C, 1D, 1S, 1C, 1D and 1T.

You are now at the centre front of the design. Work a mirror image of the sequence to reach around to the back of the design.

8 Check the necklace for size - if you need a longer necklace add more repeats of 1B, 1A to either end.

9 Finish off one end of the wire with a French crimp as on page six. Thread the second crimp onto the other end of the wire and form the loop - before you secure the crimp check that the dangles all fall properly at the front of the design - if you make the wire too tight they will not fall properly. Squeeze the crimp to secure and add the clasp with a 4mm jump ring on either side.

∽ Making the Earrings ∽

10 Make two Q dangles as on the necklace design.

11 Make two P dangles as on the necklace design. Twist open the loop on an eyepin and attach 1P. Twist the loop shut and thread on 1A, 1D, 1A and 1B. Trim and loop - call this dangle U (fig 22). Repeat to make a second identical dangle.

fig 22

Q

U

12 Attach a 4mm jump ring to the top of each of the four dangles.

13 Twist open the loop on an eyepin and attach 1Q and 1U. Twist the loop shut. Thread on 1A, 1E and 1A. Trim and make a loop IN THE SAME PLANE as the loop at the bottom of the pin.

14 Twist the loop on the earfitting open and attach the earring.

Repeat to make a mirror image earring.

A delicate swagged design that sparkles with crystals is going to be a great addition to anyone's jewellery box. Make it in pastel pinks to go with a special summer dress, ivory for a wedding day or cool blues for an evening out at the theatre. Refer to pages four and five for more information about loops, linking and jump rings.

You Will Need

2g size 10/0 seed beads A
Thirty-two 4mm pearl beads B
Five 4x6mm crystal rondelles C
Eleven 6mm pearl beads D
Seven 6x8mm crystal rondelles E
One filigree butterfly stamping
Seven headpins
Forty-eight eyepins
Forty-nine 4mm jump rings
One clasp set
A pair of earfittings

Making the Necklace

1 Thread 1A, 1B and 1A onto a headpin. Trim and loop. Attach an eyepin to this dangle and thread on 1C. Trim and loop. Attach an eyepin to the loop just made and thread on 1A, 1D and 1A. Trim and loop - make three of these linked dangles in total.

2 Take one of the dangles made in step one and attach an eyepin to the top loop. Thread on 1E. Trim and loop. Attach a new eyepin to the loop just made and thread on 1A, 1B and 2A. Trim and loop.

fig 23

3 Referring to fig 23 use a jump ring to connect the two shorter dangles to the holes marked X on the bottom of the butterfly filigree.

4 Attach a jump ring to each of the holes marked Y on fig 23. Join these two rings together with a third jump ring. Twist open the loop on the top of the long dangle made in step 2 and attach it to this third jump ring.

5 You now need to make the links for the swags and the neckchain. Each link is made onto an eyepin - you need to make sure that that the loop you make is in the SAME PLANE as the loop on the other end of the pin - this will make the chain and swags hang properly. See page five for more information about same plane. Thread 1B onto an eyepin. Trim and loop. Make twelve of these links in total and call them P.

6 Thread 1C onto an eyepin. Trim and loop - make two of these links in total and call them Q.

7 Thread 1D onto an eyepin. Trim and loop. Make six of these links in total and call them R.

8 Thread 1E onto an eyepin. Trim and make a loop. Make four of these in total and call them S.

9 Thread 2A, 1B and 2A onto an eyepin. trim and make a loop. Make twelve of these in total and call them T.

10 The Swags - using a single jump ring to make each join link together 1P, 1Q and 3P into a single length. Use a jump ring to connect the first P link to the hole marked Z on fig 23. Attach a jump ring to the other end of the length just completed.

11 Using a single jump ring link together 1R and 1S. Use a jump ring to connect the free end of the R link to the loop at the top corner of the butterfly filigree. Attach a jump ring to the free end of the S link.

12 Open a jump ring and thread on the jump rings at the end of the chains made in steps 10 and 11. Before you close the jump ring add in 1R. Close the jump ring (fig 24).

fig 24

13 Using a single jump ring for each join start to make up the neck chain from the free end of the 1R just added - start with 1P, 1S, 1P, 1R and 1T. Add four more T links.

14 Repeat from step 10 for the other side of the design. Try the necklace for size and adjust as necessary.

Add the clasp with a jump ring to either side.

∽ Making the Earrings ∾

15 Thread onto a headpin 1A, 1B and 1A. Trim and loop. Thread a second headpin with 1A, 1B and 4A. Trim and loop.

16 Twist open a jump ring and link together the loops at the top of the two prepared headpins and the loop on an eyepin. Twist the jump ring shut.

17 Thread 1E onto the pin - trim and loop. Link a new eyepin onto this loop and thread on 1D. Trim and loop. Twist open the loop on an earfitting and link onto the top of the last pin. Repeat to make a second earring.

Beader's Tip
This design uses a lot of eyepins to make lots of short links - this produces lots of offcuts. If you are confident about loop making use the offcut from the first link to make the second link etc or swap to using 0.6mm wire - it is more economical on your purse and the environment.

Juno Necklace & Earrings

This is a fabulously easy technique that grows very quickly - you can make the stamens at the front of the necklace as long as you want - these instructions will make a pendant piece approximately 55x40mm in size. There is extra information about twisting wire, using stranded beading wire, crimps, loops and jump rings on pages 4, 5, 6 and 7.

You Will Need

Sixty 4mm pearl beads A
Seven 6mm pearl beads B
28 French crimps C
Three 4mm diamante chatons
2.5m of 0.4mm soft wire
50 cm of stranded beading wire
Four 4mm jump rings
Two eyepins
One clasp set
One pair of ear fittings
A little PVA glue

Put aside
2 x 30cm of 0.4mm wire,
18A and 2B
for the earrings

Making the Necklace

1 Reserve 12 A beads for the necklace strap.
Smooth out the 0.4mm wire between your fingers. Thread on 1A and bring to the middle of the wire. Fold the wire about the bead and pinch the two sides of the wire together 35mm from the bead (fig 24).

2 Twist the wire between the bead and the pinch by turning the bead over and over (fig 25).

fig 24

fig 25

3 Separate the two wire ends. Onto the longest end thread 1A. Make a loop 30mm long from this wire with the bead at the end of the loop and the two sides of the loop coming together at the base of the previous twist (fig 26). Pinch the two sides of the loop together at the base of the previous twist and twist a new stamen (fig 27).

fig 26

fig 27

4 Separate the wire ends and onto the longest end thread 1A. Make a new 25mm loop with the A bead at the bend and the two sides of the loop coming together at the base of the previous twists. Pinch at the base of the loop and twist as before (fig 28).

fig 28

5 Choosing the longest wire end make a loop 20mm in length - do not thread on a bead. Pinch the two sides of the loop together at the base of the previous stamens and twist. As you twist the loop at the end will become smaller and smaller - stop when the loop is 3mm in diameter (fig 29).

fig 29

6 Repeat step 5 to make a second stamen 20mm long with a plain loop at the end. Arrange the stamens you have made so far as in fig 30. The long beaded stamens set the length of the pendant spray at the front, the two unbeaded stamens form two arms for the attachment of the necklace strap.

fig 30

7 You are now ready to add the remaining stamens. Always work with the longest wire end; thread on 1A and make a stamen between 8mm and 25mm in length - just make sure that the stamens all come together at the same central point as in fig 30. Build up a starburst shape with one stamen overlapping another. As you work make three more stamens, of varying length, without an A bead at the end - these stamens will hold the chatons. Leave at least 3A beads for step 8.

fig 31

8 Arrange the stamens into a pleasing shape - curve the stamens a little so they appear to drape a little. Make sure the two stamens made in Steps 5 and 6 are still in the correct place to attach the strap.
Bring both ends of the wire to the centre of the spray at the front of the work.
Onto the longest wire end thread 1B. Make a very small loop with the B bead at the end of the loop and twist to bring the B bead in tightly to the front of the spray (fig 31).
Repeat with two more B beads. Add two or three A beads into the gaps to make a tight cluster at the centre front of the spray.

9 Make sure that the spray is secure and finish off the wire ends by trimming to 5mm and tucking into the hole in one of the B beads.

10 Cut the stranded beading wire in half.
Referring to page 7 - figs 14, 15 and 16) thread onto the first length 1C, 1A and 1C. Make a loop at the end of the wire 3mm in diameter and secure with the crimps concealing the end of the wire inside the A bead. Link this loop to the first stamen loop on the pendant spray with a jump ring.

11 Thread onto this wire 1C, 1B and 1C followed by four repeats of 1C, 1A and 1C. Do not squash these crimps yet. Referring to step 5 on page 7 thread on 1C and set the length of this necklace strap. Thread on a further 1A and 1C to complete the strap making the loop at the end as in fig 18 on page 7.

12 Repeat to make the other side strap for the design. Add the clasp set with a further jump ring on each side. Distribute the beads on the straps evenly and secure the crimps once you are happy with the design.

13 Make sure that the three blank loop stamens that you made for the chatons are facing forwards and the loops have a nice round shape. Wipe a film of PVA glue over the loops and drop in the chatons - leave to dry for two hours before handling.

∽ Juno Earrings ∾

14 Thread 1A into the middle of a 30cm length of 0.4mm wire. Pinch a loop 10mm long and twist. Repeat to make five more twists from the same central point. Make the twists between 7mm and 9mm long - each with 1A at the end. Make a final twist 8mm long without an A bead at the end - the cluster will hang from this looped stamen.

15 Arrange the stamens into a flat starburst shape with the longest stamen opposite the looped stamen. Use the wire ends to attach 1A to the centre front and 1A to the centre back of the starburst. Make sure the wire shape is secure and trim both ends neatly. Hide the raw ends inside one of the central A beads.

16 Attach an eyepin to the looped stamen and thread on 1B. Trim the pin to your desired length - the picture shows the pin left a little longer than normal to make a more elegant earring.

Save the trimming so you can measure it against the second earring pin.

Make a loop at the top of the trimmed pin and attach an earfitting.

Repeat to make the second earring.

∾◈ Gloria Finger Ring ◈∽

A quick and easy ring that is comfortable to wear. Try it with pearls instead of crystals, use six different colours of crystal or alternate pearl and crystal beads for a different look every time.

1 Gently stretch the flower filigree a little so the A beads will just fit between the petals.

2 Thread 1A into the middle of the wire. Pass the ends of the wire in opposite directions through adjacent petals on the flower and pull to bring the bead into the gap (fig 32).

fig 32

3 Thread 1A onto each end of the wire and pass through the next petal loops. Repeat to add beads four and five. Cross the wire ends over inside the sixth A bead and pull it into the last gap (fig 33).

You Will Need
One 15mm twisted filigree flower link
Six 6x4mm crystal rondelles A
1g of size 10/0 seed beads B
30cm of stranded beading wire
Two French crimps

4 Thread 6B onto each wire end. Bring the wire ends together and thread together through approximately 22B to make the shank.

5 Separate the ends and thread 6B onto each end. Pass the ends in opposite directions through the first A bead to close up the shank (fig 34). Check the ring for fit and adjust the 22B if necessary.

fig 34

fig 33

6 Thread one crimp onto each end of the wire and secure as tightly as you can up close to the A bead - tuck the crimp inside the wire petal to conceal.

Diana Bracelet

Using 0.4mm wire for this weave makes the bracelet quite firm so it sits like a narrow cuff on the wrist. Keep the wire smooth as you work and the weave is as easy as pie.

fig 35

fig 36

fig 37

1 Cut the wire in half. Thread 8A into the centre of the first length. Thread 1C onto one end of the wire and hold 2cm from the end. Pick up the other end of the wire and pass through the bead in the opposite direction (fig 35). Pull on both ends of the wire to bring the bead to the centre of the wire (fig 36). Repeat with the other piece of wire.

2 Use a bit of tape to stick the two loops down to a surface in front of you so they lie closely together and parallel. You will have two outside wires and two inside wires (fig 37).

3 Thread 1A onto each of the four wire ends. Bring the two inside wires together and thread both through 1B. Thread 1B onto each of the outside wires. Thread 1A onto each of the four wire ends (fig 38).

4 Thread 1D onto one of the outside wires and hold 2cm from the end. Pick up the closest inside wire and pass through the D bead in the opposite direction (fig 39). Pull down to the A beads. Repeat with the other pair of wires. You will notice that the wire ends from the outside are the new inside wires and vice versa. Repeat step 3.

You Will Need

2g of size 10/0 seed beads A
5g of size 3 bugles B
Sixteen 4mm pearl beads C
Fourteen 6x4mm crystal rondelle beads D
2.5m of 0.4mm soft wire
Six 4mm jump rings
A clasp set

fig 38

fig 39

fig 40

5 Onto one of the outside wires thread 1A, 1C and 1A and hold 2cm from the end. Pick up the closest inside wire and pass through these three beads in the opposite direction (fig 40). Pull down to the previous A beads. Repeat with the other pair of wires. Repeat step 3.

6 Repeat steps 4 and 5 until you have used up all of the C and D beads or the length is long enough for your wrist.

7 Thread 8A onto one of the outside wires. Pass this end through the last C bead on that side of the bracelet again to make a loop to match the 8A loop at the other end of the design. Repeat with the other outside wire.

8 Carefully wrap each wire between their adjacent A and C beads just once to secure. Pass the ends of the wire through a few A or B beads to neaten before trimming very closely.

9 Attach a jump ring to each of the 8A bead loops. At each end of the bracelet bring the two jump rings together with a third jump ring and attach the clasp.

Gloria Necklace & Earrings

You need to be precise when you are making this design but the effect is worth it. Make it in white to really dazzle or swap the crystals for pearls for a more subtle effect. Before you start read through pages 6 and 7 for more information about using crimps and stranded beading wire.

Making the Necklace

You Will Need

1g of size 10/0 seed beads A
2g of size 3 bugle beads B
Sixteen 4mm pearl beads C
Twenty one 6x8mm crystal rondelles D
Eleven 6mm pearl beads E
2.3m of stranded wire beading thread
44 French crimps F
One clasp set
One pair of earfittings

1 Cut 60 cm of wire for the main neck strand. Referring to figs 14, 15 and 16 on page 7 thread 1F, 1E and 1F onto the end of the wire and make a secure loop for the end of the design.

2 Thread onto the neck length 1F, 1D and 1F seven times.
DO NOT SQUEEZE THESE CRIMPS YET.

Referring to step 5 on page 7 thread on 1F to set the length of the necklace. Add 1E and 1F to finish off this end of the necklace with a loop.

3 Add the clasp to the loops just made with jump rings - leave the clasp closed as it will make it easier to position the beads along the main part of the design.

4 Cut 7 x 20cm of wire. Thread the first length through the 1F, 1D and 1F at the centre of the main string. Make sure the bead is in the centre of the necklace, the crimps are tight to the sides of the bead and the short length is sticking out by equal amounts to either side of the bead (fig 41). Squeeze the crimps to secure the arrangement.

fig 41

5 Repeat step four with the first D beads to either side of the central D bead. Leave a 15mm gap from the central bead, thread a 30cm length of wire through the 1F, 1D and 1F combination and squeeze the crimps.

6 Repeat step 5 with the next two beads out to either side - this time leave a gap of 20mm. Repeat again with the last D beads to either side leaving a gap of 25mm.

7 The short wires now come together into pairs. Fig 41 shows how the wires pair up - they are shown on different colours so you can see them more easily. Note how the wires coming from the left always cross over the wires from the right - this simple weave helps to prevent the design from twisting. Bring the wires together in the pairs as shown - push each pair of ends through 1E and 1F just loosely for now - DO NOT SQUEEZE THE CRIMPS YET.

fig 41

8 Make sure the necklace is fastened at the back and lay the design out in a circle. Gently adjust the wires so that the centre E bead is sitting 20mm below the central D bead and the wires that support it are making a symmetrical V shape. Now gently move out to either side positioning the next E beads 15mm below the corresponding D beads. The next E beads to either side of the centre need to sit 12mm below the second D beads to either side. DO NOT SQUEEZE THE CRIMPS YET.

9 The last pair of wires is a little different - gently adjust the outer wires on each side so they come down through the E bead without distorting the main necklace string. When all 7E beads are in the correct place squeeze the crimps to hold them in place.

10 Start the dangling strands at the centre front. Thread 1B, 1A, 1D, 1A, 1C, 1A and 1F onto each wire end. Decide how long you want the dangles to be and secure the crimps below the bottom A beads. Trim off the excess wire.

11 Repeat step 10 on the wire ends hanging from the next two pairs of D beads to either side of the centre front.

12 For the last pair to either side trim off the shortest wire snugly against the crimp below the E bead. Thread the same bead sequence onto the remaining wire end and secure at your preferred position.

ꕶ Making the Earrings ꕶ

13 Cut 15cm of wire. Bring the two ends together and pass through 1E, 1A, 1D and 1F. Push the combination up towards the middle of the wire until you are left with just 4mm loop of wire showing (fig 42). Squeeze the crimp to secure the beads.

14 Thread 1B, 1A, 1C and 1A onto each wire end. Decide how long you want the strands to be and squeeze the crimps to secure the beads. Trim away the excess wire neatly.

fig 42

15 Add an earfitting to the top loop and repeat to make a second earring.

～∞⬦∞～ Artemis Necklace & Earrings ～∞⬦∞～

A stylish design to set off a tailored dress or make it in pastel shades and use an organza ribbon tie for the clasp for a soft summery look. Refer to pages 4, 5, 6 and 7 for more information about the techniques used here.

You Will Need

3g of size 10/0 seed beads A
One hundred & twenty 6mm pearl beads B
Forty one 4mm pearl beads C
Three 6x8mm crystal rondelles D
One flower shaped casting
Six chatons to set in the casting
Five headpins & nine eyepins
Four French crimps E
1.2m of stranded beading wire
1.5m of 0.4mm soft wire
Five 4mm & one 6mm
jump ring
One pair of earfittings
One clasp set
A little PVA glue

Making the Necklace

1 Cut the stranded wire in half. Thread onto the first piece 4A, 1B, 3A, 1B, 2A and 1B. Now thread on 19 repeats of 1A and 1B. Follow this sequence with 10A and 31 repeats of 1B and 1A. Thread on 1B, 2A, 1B, 3A, 1B and 4A. Put this row aside for a moment.

2 Thread onto the second length of stranded wire 2A, 1B, 3A, 1B, 2A and 1B. Now thread on 18 repeats of 1A and 1B. Thread on 4A. Lay this wire alongside the first wire so the beads just threaded lie parallel to the 19 repeats of 1A and 1B on the first length. Pass the end of the new wire through the middle 2A beads of the 10A on the first strand (fig 43).

3 Thread 4A onto the new wire followed by 28 repeats of 1B and 1A. Thread on 1A, 1B, 3A, 1B and 2A.

4 Lay the two rows parallel. Pass both wires at one end through 1E. Repeat at the other end. Try the pearly necklace for size - if you want to add/remove beads from the length do so now and replace the 1E crimps. Squeeze the crimps flat to secure the rows. At one end of the design trim away the shortest wire as closely as possible. Thread 1B and 1E onto the remaining wire. Bend the wire back through the 1E and 1B to make a loop. Draw the loop down to 3mm and squeeze the 1E crimp to secure. Trim away the excess wire, repeat at the other side of the design and attach your fastener.

fig 43